Everything About EBay Selling: Unlock EBay Financial Prowess

M A Muoghalu

ISBN-13: 978-1481889001
ISBN-10: 1481889001

DEDICATION

Dedicated to the honor of all the single parents out there and indeed to every man
and woman who works hard every single day to feed a child or take care of a
family. To the honor of all those good people who have found the niche to
financial independence and are willing to help others climb the same lather. To that
person who take a minute out of his or her time to stop the vehicle, roll down the
window to offer a dollar bill to that beggar at the traffic stop or by the road-side
without any pre-judgment. This book is dedicated to all of you, the unsung heroes
good tidings.

CONTENTS

ACKNOWLEDGMENTS

In appreciation to God Almighty the ultimate knowledge, the ultimate wisdom, the ultimate power, the ultimate truth, the only reality there is and the source of every other, the omnipresent, omnipotent and omniscient, for His ever-abiding love and grace in me through His only Son; our Lord and Savior Jesus Christ.

1. INTRODUCTION

In 2003, it was predicted, statistically, that the number of online U.S shoppers will double to 132 million. It happened exactly as predicted. Look at the following statistics from 2007 - 2012:

Year 2007   No. of online shoppers: 133.1 million

Year 2008   No. of online shoppers: 138.5 million

Year 2009   No. of online shoppers: 143.7 million

Year 2010   No. of online shoppers: 148.7 million

Year 2011   No. of online shoppers: 153.5 million

Year 2012   No. of online shoppers: 158.2 million

If you study the above statistics closely you will discover there is average increment of online shoppers each year by 5 million shoppers. Bad or stagnant economy does not deter consumers who enjoy the convenience of doing their shopping from the comfort of their individual homes. 63% of online shoppers are women and people with kids are more likely to shop online than people without children. So if you are considering selling online, there's never been a better time to start and take advantage of these million shoppers with tons of moneys looking for products to buy. You can open a website or build your own online store but you have to do a heck of promotions, advertisement and infomercials to drive traffic for consumers to notice and become aware of your online store. However, even when some consumers do become aware of your site, there's still the trust issue and that lack of confidence on the shoppers in terms of the authenticity of your website and safety of their personal information. The greatest fear online shoppers have is the fear of fraud and scam - identity theft and hijackers. Therefore if you want to sell online and you are a beginner, it's better to start out selling your products or services with an established site, an online marketplace with a proven and track record of excellence, an online auction giant so popular it's being used by people all over and across the globe, from Africa to Europe, from North to South America, from Asia to Australia all the way to the beautiful valleys of Oceania. We are talking about **EBAY.COM**

EBay is still one of the leading giants in online marketplace. Its competitors cannot come an inch closer. There are lots of online auction marketplaces today on the internet, from overstock.com to amazon.com to quickbid.com and a whole bunch of others. EBay has developed both name and reputation worldwide and statistically proven to be an unmatched force for the success of many of its online sellers across the globe with sea of sellers, ocean of goods and river of buyers all around the world. The financial potential with eBay is endless. It's real, it works, and it's never a scam. I am a living witness and testimony of how one who is committed to selling on eBay can achieve a substantial financial success. Millions and billions of dollars are being circulated on eBay each year in transactions. Smart sellers take advantage of this and tap into this ocean of wealth.

Due to the name, reputation and financial success potential on eBay, a lot of people are selling on eBay, many more striving to get started. There are no limits on what you can sell or make on eBay, though there are restrictions on items like firearms, ammunitions, weapons and dangerous materials. EBay auction is classified in three: 1). eBay motors -meant for listing, selling and trading automobiles and related items. 2). eBay classified - portion meant for selling real estate, digital and informational products. This section is actually made of kijiji.com, online real estate selling and trading interactive site purchase and incorporated by eBay. 3) everything else or general auction - this is the portion of eBay where you list and sell every other products other than the ones already listed above. This section is where majority of sellers and buyers on eBay visit very often and where you are most likely to be selling on eBay.

If you were to make some money on eBay selling, you have to be, not just an informed seller, but also one who is well-informed, who knows, understands and masters the rules and policies that guide eBay auction and marketplace activities. There are thousands of books and programs out there; in the bookstores, on CDs, DVDs and over the internet, quick to introduce people to eBay selling but hardly do you find one that really exposes, addresses and expatiates on the fine-prints of eBay fees, rules and policies to help those become well-informed sellers, make wise decisions, be better prepared, help them better anticipate and articulate what they are getting into, thereby giving them a better head start, well-equipped to beat the competition fresh out of box.

Think of this as an investment and what do you

understand by investment? Generally, investment is whatever cause you put your money, time or effort in for a beneficial result or outcome. You do not just invest your hard-earned money on something without first acquiring the necessary knowledge about that investment that will help you consider the pros and cons, articulate hurdles, weigh options and be able to predict the possible outcome. Selling on eBay is the way to go folks. You will be investing your money, time, energy and effort in it so you need to understand the policies and rules that guide eBay auction marketplace to make you an informed eBay seller. Being an informed eBay seller will help you make the most and the best out of eBay. We are all selling on eBay to make money, but if you do not know, understand and properly master the basic seller rules and read in-between the fine prints, sorry to say this, but you will end up loosing. I'm a living witness. Remember what they say: 'Experience is the best teacher'. I learnt the hard way. At the time I was so excited to get started selling on eBay after I purchased and read a few books about eBay selling and auction, I thought I had known everything I needed to make a lot of cash on eBay. The books gave me basic knowledge about selling on eBay but none mentioned anything about the outrageous and excessive eBay fees or the eBay market police (strict rules and policies). I guess the authors of those books either do not think it as important or just want to leave the poorly informed potential eBay sellers at their own fate of luck and chance in terms of result. I never knew there are fees I suppose to pay for listing on eBay. It's not just a few fees, there are innumerous of those. I never knew all the fees I was charged for listing my items on eBay has nothing to do with the one I would be charged when the item finally sells, known as the Final Value Fee. EBay has long teamed up with pay pal for almost all the financial transactions of its customers (sellers and buyers alike). Pay pal also charges its own fees for using their service to complete your financial transactions on eBay. This means you have to have an account with pay pal too if you were to sell or buy on eBay.

None of these books I read said anything about pay pal transactions, and it's imperative I know about pay pal transactions and how it works, and the catch, if any. These and similar information put together make you a better informed eBay seller. Getting a firm grip and a good handle on this knowledge and all these pieces of information helps jumpstart and give your eBay selling business a head start. Eventually I listed my first item on eBay based on the basic knowledge I had by reading a few books. To fast forward and cut the long story short, I finally got the listing process right but found out at the end that I had acquired a bunch of fees just on one successfully listed item. This is not all that is to it, before I could click on the'list your item' button at the bottom of the page, there is another fine print which says that despite all the listing fees I was charged, there is going to be a final value fee charged if the listed item eventually sells.

The problem here is very clear; assuming you want to list 30 or more items on eBay and it cost $2.50 for your item to be listed. Now multiply 30 (number of items) by $2.50 (cost to list an item), this is going to given you a total of $75. This fee you will pay whether the item sells or not and there is no guarantee any or all of the items are going to sell before or by the end of the selected auction period which ranges from 1 day till up to 10 days. Keep in mind the fees only cover for the selected auction duration. EBay charges monthly, so assuming you list 30 items for $2.50 each for a duration of 10 days but it happens that some or none of the items is sold when the auction ends, you will have to re-list them again for the same fee amount to keep selling or at least trying to get them sold. That's going to attract another sets of listing fees in addition to the one you have already accrued. This means within the monthly billing period, you may find your account racking up to $125 just on listing fees alone. You probably may have succeeded in selling some of these items but the fee you end up acquiring on the listings alone on those items is more than the profit you make on them and does so with such a great margin. So it's imperative you understand eBay fees and it's charged. Listing your item does not guarantee any sales. This does not mean your item get lost in the midst of thousands of similar items, rather you probably need to retouch on your description and listing criteria. This book teaches you all of that.

Remember what we said earlier about pay pal. Every financial transaction you're doing on eBay should be through pay pal whether buying an item or selling a product. It turns out pay pal also charges sellers for every transaction. Therefore understanding all these auction fees and policies, when and how they're charged help make you a better informed eBay seller and will help you get a handle on what really transpires behind the auction scene, which, to a great extent will determine your success or failure selling on eBay. This book is all about exposing those fine prints you need to know and be aware of as a potential eBay seller to make better informed decisions and not start out loosing from day one.

I have put together, my seven solid years of experience selling and buying on eBay for you so you can learn from my mistakes and also capitalize on my success to make the most and best out of your eBay investment selling. It's usually said that experience is the best teacher, however, in this age of internet and information, you do not have to wait until you experience failure and setbacks before picking up your success. Learn from the stories and accounts of those who have already walked the walk and been there before you, willing to share such experience with you either in form of e-books, books, video courses, etc. Any amount spent to get niche information about your aspiration is part of your investment. **'Knowledge is Power'** says the American **Francis Bacon**. You need to do whatever you can to acquire and have it in whatever you do.

May be you already have an account with eBay and ready to start selling, may be not. It's okay because this book will walk you through from the entrance all the way to the exit. Everything you to know about selling on eBay as far as the basic seller rules, policies and fees are concerned: the guidelines, basic auction policy and rules, fees, listings and listing features, bids, offers, ending auction, transaction cancellation, disputes and resolutions, feedbacks and how it works in improving your seller performance rating/standard, and a lot more. After reading this book and digesting the information in it properly, you are guaranteed to acquire the skill and mastery to start selling on eBay like a pro because in this book no stone is going to be left unturned on whatever it is that you need to know about selling on eBay that will make you a smart and well informed seller. You will understand how to eliminate risks and losses upfront, master basic very important auction fees/rules so you can get the most out of eBay and start winning from day one and not loosing. So if you are ready to take this bull by the horn, your opportunity is right here, right now, in your face knocking. If you are ready and willing to open your door to this opportunity of your financial freedom and success selling on eBay like millions of sellers on eBay are doing even as you are thinking right now about starting, then do not stop here. Get the book with the entire information and start right away, generating tons of cash on eBay. Always remember, one of the secrets of you successfully selling items on eBay lies on your **ad and listings description** and in this book I give you the anatomy of an excellent listings ad and show stopper item description guaranteed to get the attention and interest of your potential buyers.

2. GETTING STARTED

DETERMININIG WHAT TO SELL ON EBAY:

Almost anything that has some value to it sells on eBay. Don't worry about how old or new, used or right out of box it appears. There is someone out there who for some reason want that old worn out item you have in your garage or closet. EBay has ocean, and I mean ocean of buyers from all around the globe: from North to South America, Africa to Europe, Asia to Australia, extending all the way to the beautiful valleys of the Oceania continent. I have had buyers from places I have never read, heard or knew existed. That's how diverse and huge eBay buyers are from all peoples, cultures, beliefs and civilization. You can start selling on eBay by cleaning up your house, garage, closet or storage. However, I assume am providing this information to potential full time eBay investors/sellers, people who wish to make their living selling on eBay, seeking to find financial success through it. Since you will be selling on eBay to make substantial profit, it's extremely important you start by finding out what is it to list and sell that will attract buyers, bids and sell sooner than later because that's where your cash is.

There are few ways to research for hot selling items on any category on eBay that are in demand, items people are scrambling to beat the auction to purchase. One of the ways is by using terapeak.com. This is a website that utilizes eBay integration software developed to analyze and give you an inside scoop into the activities of eBay market auction. The site is not free though. They charge for membership which is of two levels. First level, which comes with limited access, is $29.99/month. This level only provides you with information about the selling and buying activities on ebay.com (limited only to U.S buyers and sellers). Second level or level 2 cost a bit more but will provide you with information on the selling and buying activities on all of the eBay auction site from eBay U.S to eBay Canada, China, UK, and to the rest of eBay international auction sites, including on eBay motors. However, you're most likely to not need the second level of membership unless you wish to be selling on these other eBay sites. Everything you need to be successful selling on eBay is there on your local eBay site and the buyers visiting are not restricted, they are from all over the world. Therefore you do not have to list on all these sites for you to be selling internationally.

When you have access to terapeak.com you will see the

statistics and analytical data on what items on any category have higher sales rate at any given point in time and which items in any category have hottest appeal on buyers. Working with this tool gives you a good head start and boosts your confidence knowing that you are selling items statistically proven to have substantial consumer demands on eBay. Demand as we know it drives the market. If demand is high on an item, it means that if you have and list that particular item for sale (taking into account the brand, model and features), you will make profit because it's going to sell. Terapeak.com takes the guess out of the work for you. I strongly recommend their services to anyone selling or wishing to start selling on eBay, and if you are reading this book right now, it means am strongly recommending it to you. Go to terapeak.com to learn more. It's okay to pause your reading for a minute and visit the site and return later because a sneak peak into the services offered by this website will definitely help fan your enthusiasm about selling and making money on eBay.

There is also another way you can figure out what's hot and in high demand in any category on eBay. It's eBay's own tool known as the **'Completed Listings'**. When you open an eBay site, on the top of the page is the search field, at the right end of the search field are two words that read: **'advanced search'** link. Click on it, select the category you want to search in, scroll down to **"Search including"**, click to check on the **'completed listing'** box, scroll further down to **"Buying formats"**, click to check on **'auction'** box. Scroll even further down to **"Sort by"** click on the field that says **'Best Match'** and select **'price: highest first'**, then click on search. The search field will display all the completed listings of the items in that category. Some of the prices will be displayed in red and some in green color. The items with their prices displayed in red are items listed that never sold or not sold yet. However those items with their prices displayed in green are items listed that sold. This means therefore, you'll need to pay attention to items with prices displayed in green, with particular attention to the number of bids the item has before it got sold, as shown before the price, because that's where your cash is, items sold with up to 20 bids or more. That's where your money making opportunity lies, if you can find and list similar items, paying greater attention to the brand, model and features of the item(s) in question. Look for those items sold with higher number of bids (double digit bids). Why? Because it means that item is in great demand and a lot of consumers are up for it, wanting to purchase it while the supply remains low no matter the quantity put up for sale. All you need to do is to find the same exact item, taking the ones sold as shown in the completed listings as your model. How do you find the same items? Easy. Google it, put it on Google search engine and from there you will find stores or sellers that sell same exact item. Please do your due diligence, do you research well. Please pay particular attention to the features possessed by your model items, this is extremely important and I will explain. Assuming you used the completed listings and discovered that all the listings on this particular book sold for not less than $1,500.00 with a lot of bids, and you Google, find similar book and put it up for sale in the same category and no one cares to bid on it, you'll start wondering what the heck is different between the one you listed and those other ones listed that sold for a lot more money. Look closely; there is something yours is lacking compares to the ones sold as shown on the completed listings. May be they're autographed by the authors - meaning that the authors of those books personally signed those books. That signature alone is the difference between $10.00 and $1000.00 May be those books are first editions or first prints or combination of both. So these are the details you really have to pay attention to before finding your own to sell. If you don't, you will be very disappointed. Those autographs, special prints and first editions make those other books highly collectible. The values of collectible items are timeless, and antique collectibles gets better with age.

3. FINDING ITEMS TO SELL ON EBAY

PERSONAL ITEMS: As I said previously in this book, finding items to sell on eBay is just as close as cleaning up your house, closet or garage and putting those up on eBay for auction or with fixed pricing if your are sure of the value and price of your item as far as FMV (Fair Market Value) is concerned. There are also some other ways to find items to sell on eBay. You can use your own money to purchase items from a supplier or wholesaler at considerably lower price reselling those for substantial profit. If you have money in your pocket and you are considering doing this, I will suggest you go liquidation.com where you can buy a whole bunch or bulk of items far much less than usual and turn around to resell those for a reasonable amount of money with tangible profit.

CRAIGSLIST.ORG: This is one of the hottest person to person online transaction community available where people post a lot of items for sale, personal items, private and professional sellers alike. Each seller calls his or her own shots on craigslist. There are lots of desperate sellers on craigslist willing and ready to sell their highly valued items for pennies on a dollar either to get the money to solve some personal issue or just to get rid of it. The opportunity with craigslist is limitless. Use the eBay completed listings tool as explained earlier on to find hot selling item you may be interested in and find that on craigslist for less, buy it and re-list it on eBay.com using the principles and guidelines in this book to catch in big. I have written a book solely dedicated making huge profits and catching in on craigslist's items by selling them on eBay.com and amazon,com. Check it out. **Mam-merchandise.com**

Yard sales, **Salvation Army**, **Value Village**, **thrift stores** and **Goodwill** are all places you can find items to sell on eBay. The reason is that you buy items here for up to 70% less than what you may probably buy them at regular stores, and sell them with humongous profits on eBay. The secret here is where you can buy things extremely cheap and resell those with huge profit on eBay.

CHINESE SOURCING: You can also look into what I call the 'China Buzz' - China sourcing. Most items people sell on eBay and other online auctions are merchandise made and ordered from China. Even the off-line stores, both big and small import majority of their items from China. Even in our daily politics and economic news reports, we hear often about how a lot U.S companies are exporting their productions, whole or part of it to China. The labor is extremely cheap compared to the U.S workers and the output is enormous. Go to dhgate.com or alibaba.com to learn more and explore all the options. These sites are for China sourcing, however do your due diligence, do your research very well. It's always good to buy generic goods when doing China sourcing. Never buy products with brand name identification from China because 9 out of 10, chances are, they are counterfeits. China sourcing is only good for generic goods without brand name tag. For example, if you purchase an apple I-pad from China, it's going to be up to three times cheaper than ones purchased from any U.S authorized seller. Both products will look just the same in appearance and visible features, but the problem lies in the system and software compatibility. It won't take you time to figure out that some or almost all the Apple Apps needed to install to work with the gadget system are virtually incompatible with the one purchased at ridiculously low price from China. This means you will loose big time if you happen to find yourself in this type of situation. Customers who purchase such from you will eventually seek for return and refund. Therefore to avoid this, it's a lot better not to buy items for sale from China that have some brand name label on them because though the physical appearance may be same, system compatibility is completely different.

You can own a warehouse full of goods purchased at a very low cost from China. It's an easy and convenient way to start one's own business, however do your research and be sure the product(s) is a **niche** item, something people really wanted. Since you will probably be selling on eBay, use the research tools earlier on suggested and explained. You may want to revisit that column and be sure you properly read, understood and digested the information.

*WARNING: Never buy any products with brand names from China, rather buy generic merchandise. This I already explained above.

So let's get back to finding items to sell on eBay. The next one is my most and all time favorite when it comes to selling items on eBay. It's what's commonly known as DROPSHIPPING.

4. DROPSHIPPING

This is a great way to list and sell items on eBay, almost any items of your choice without even lifting a finger or spending a dime on any of them. So what exactly is drop-shipping? Let me explain this with an analogy. Take for instance you want to sell a particular MP3 player on eBay and have already done all your research with 'terapeak.com' and/or with eBay 'Completed Listings' and have concluded with statistical facts that this particular MP3 player has reasonable consumer demand. Your next step is to find a seller of that particular item or a few similar sellers just to help with price comparisms. Go to **www.wholesalecentral.com** and find lists of wholesalers who sell that particular item you looking at well discounted prices, choose seller that offer you the lowest price and best discount. You can also type in the word 'wholesale' on Google search engine and thousands of those will show up. However, be careful. Be sure to do your **due diligence** and research because some of those sellers who claim to be wholesalers are mere regular retailers. This means when you purchase from them, they will buy from the real wholesalers who in turn will drop-ship to your customers. So find a wholesaler who sells this item cheap enough that you can still increase the selling price (without over-pricing it) and be able to sell it and make substantial profit. Take into consideration, the ridiculous eBay seller/listing fees and pay pal transaction charges, in case your item sells. I will explain more about these fees in later chapters in this book. Now that you find the right item with the right wholesaler, all you need to do is list the item on eBay in the right category with proper pictures and right description. Pay attention to details about the product condition - new, used, like new, good, refurbished, etc. Features, quantity and use should all be well described in clear and uncompromising or misleading details.

If the item sells and the money is in your pay pal account, of course you will know this because Pay-Pal will send you an email notification about payment received with few details, print the details of the transaction either from your paypal account homepage or from your eBay account. I personally verify payment with my paypal account but print the transaction details from eBay because for me eBay's is more detailed than pay-pal's and that serves as my receipt to my buyers for the transaction. Equipped with this information then, go to your wholesaler web-store and place an order for that particular item you sold at the price being sold by the wholesaler. Now I want you to pay serious attention because this is where DROPSHIPPING is going to be initiated and activated, if you prefer to use that word. Usually when you make a purchase on almost any online stores and web businesses, during the payment process, usually two addresses are requested from you on check-out: a). the billing address and, b). the shipping address. Billing address is usually the same address you registered your account with your financial institution and both address must match for the transaction to be authorized by your bank. Shipping address on the other hand is the address where you would want the item to be mailed, shipped or sent to, by the seller. I guess you are beginning to get the picture now. So enter your personal address on the billing column, which of course suppose to match with the one you registered with your financial institution for them to verify and authorize your transaction, and then enter your customer's address as detailed on transaction page on eBay or pay-pal which you suppose to have printed out for reference, on the shipping column. BINGO!!! That's it. When the seller processes your transaction, he or she can only ship to the address as indicated on the shipping address column, meaning that your seller will be shipping directly to your buyer. You can do this with about every transaction and about any product you want to sell on eBay.

This exactly was how I personally started selling on eBay and raised enough cash to order my own niche items and start shipping from the comfort and convenience of my own backyard. That is why this book has little or nothing to do with what I read or researched but rather a child born out of pure experience, experience emanating from my rolled sleeves and hands constantly on the job. Everything am writing in this book are things I personally did and still do, experienced, been through, had a sleepless night over, cracked my brains about it, came up with solutions, put them in practical use and evaluate results through feasible facts and known statistics. I am teaching you the same thing and process without letting any stones unturned. These guidelines if followed and properly integrated, is guaranteed to enhance your eBay selling experience, it doesn't matter if you are a pro or a newbie, it's guaranteed to maximize your profit potentials on eBay starting from day one. Drop-shipping is the way to go and it's never hard a process to follow. **The steps are as easy as 1-2-3. Step 1**: Find your niche products through research - (using terapeak.com tools and from eBay completed listings, preferably). **Step 2**: Find a wholesaler or supplier of the niche product, compare prices and be sure you get those at highest discount possible to enable you increase the price without overpricing it and sell with substantial profit, taken all listing fees and pay-pal charges into consideration. **Step 3**: During check out with your wholesaler, after the item sold on eBay, be sure to type in your personal address on the Billing Address Column and type in your buyer's address in the column that says 'Shipping Address'. That's it, you done. This method of selling is the door that truly ushered me to eBay marketplace. At the time I was desperate to earn extra income selling on eBay. I did my eBay market analysis, figured out what I would sell but just did not have enough cash to order the products to start selling. That was when I started storming the internet to gather every piece of information I could possibly find about selling on eBay, and in the process came to find out about DROPSHIPPING. That piece of information helped changed my life for better. It was like finding a missing key to the door of financial success. Ever since then, I never looked back and nothing has been able to stop me. I hope and wish that, after reading this book, you may neither look back nor allow anything to stop you.

This is by far the best way to sell on eBay especially if you have little or no cash at all to purchase your own goods for sale. However, like every other process, drop-shipping has its own technicalities, guidelines and rules to be followed to get the best out of it. These are things you need to understand and take into consideration when using drop-shipping for your sales. The invoice your wholesaler sends will bear your personal information; name and address to your buyer and not the seller's. This is cool but it has some implications in terms of returning items. If after the item is drop-shipped to your buyer, by the wholesaler from whom you ordered and your buyer for some reason decides to return the item back either for exchange or refund, the customer will be returning it to you not to the wholesaler who drop-shipped it to them. You in turn will ship it back to your wholesaler. This therefore means that you have to be careful and be sure the return policy you stipulated in your listing of that particular item on eBay properly compliments with that of your wholesaler who sells to you and drop-ships to your customers, so you wouldn't have any issues returning the items back to you seller if your customer decides to return for exchange or refund. Everyone will be on the same page in terms of return policy. This is one of the many areas you need to be smart and make use of your common sense. But I have already done the work and the thinking for you, all you have to do now is to make sure you read and digest the information properly and follow the guidelines. So take for instance your wholesaler has his return policy set within **7 business days**, have yours set within **3 business days**. This way the customer will return it to you and you in turn will have the time you need to return it to your wholesaler. This means your wholesaler returns the item within 3 business days as stipulated in your return policy on eBay, you will have 4 business days to return it to your wholesaler, and when you add it all up, it still gives you 7 business days which complies with the return policy of your wholesaler. It will be all win-win-win situation for your buyer, you and your wholesaler. Therefore whatever the number of days your wholesaler's return policy covers on any item, make sure yours is at least 4 days short of his. COMPREDEZ??? Of course return policy covers both exchange and refund. If your wholesaler does not offer refund on an item, do not offer refund on that particular item when listing it on eBay for sale and assuming no one is going to ask you for refund. Please do not assume anything. Take rules and policies seriously, they're there for your protection. If you ignore, neglect or think you can avoid it, it will definitely find and hunt you someday, somewhere, somehow.

Drop-shipping is by far the best way to sell on eBay without owning any of the items you selling. However I will encourage you to build your own warehouse (using China sourcing), start ordering and shipping your own products. It may not save you time because of the processing and shipping involved given the number of orders you receive but it will definitely save you a lot of money and increase your profit potentials. If your wholesaler sells you a product for $35.00, be assured he ordered those from the supplier in question, way much less and cheaper than it's sold because he has to make his own substantial profit on your transactions with him. It's simple business acumen, until product reaches the final consumer, it will continue to generate profit at the hands of every seller who purchases with the intention of re-selling to someone else. In my **special eBay sales report**, I will teach and show you how to sell and drop-ship on eBay with amazon.com. It's interesting and you need to get excited about it. There has not been any author or that many books that have really touched bases on this type of selling on eBay, where you can sell your items on eBay but use amazon.com to fulfill the transaction effortlessly. I give the special report free with the purchase of this book but you have to request your own copy of the report from me before I can send it to you. This means if you don't request for it, you will not get it. Remember I sell the report independently and make some money out of it, so am not all that excited to give it away free. Now you understand why I said if you don't request for it, you definitely will not get it.

SELLING ANTIQUES AND COLLECTIBLES ITEMS WITH COMPLETED LISTINGS: Now listen up! because if you can give your time and do this right and properly, you are guaranteed to generate tens if not thousands of hundreds of dollars selling on eBay. What is this? It's selling antiques and collectibles on eBay, but it's not any kind of antiques or collectibles. What you need to sale is already there for you, all you need to do is to scour your house, community, internet, flea markets, yard sales, place ads, do whatever you need to do to find any or some of these items, and you are guaranteed to sale those as soon as you put them up for sale on eBay because the buyers of these items are emptying their pockets bidding on these items whenever any appears for auction. So what are some of these antiques items? It could be anything. These are certain old paintings, drawings, books, newspapers, magazines, images, attire, devices, instruments, etc, the list is endless. Go to antiques and collectible section on EBay to see it all. There are also collectibles. Things like autographed items, sports memorabilia, trading cards, images, figurines, books, or anything collectors figure would rise in value over times because of either the time it's made, or the limited quantity of it, or the personality behind such items. Like I said earlier, they are collecting these items because the conditions surrounding them will make them will retain and definitely increase their monetary value over time. Just think of the **Amazing Spider Man's comic book** sold for cents in the **1930's,** recently sells on eBay auction for **$150,000.00.** Similar item sold on offline auction for over **$200,000.00.** Hard to believe, but believe it. Later in this book I show you how to use the completed listings tool to search out all the good selling items on Ebay, from any secion or category. All you need to do is use the completed listing tools I showed you earler to pull the niche product on any category of your interest, see what it's selling for and how exactly it's been sold, then go find it, list it and cash in. There is no magic or empty claim in this one, or promise of unrealistic money making claims to get you excited. This is as pragmatic as it can get. Completed listing tools lets you view any sold item with the price, date and most importantly the number of buyers who bid on it before it got sold. This means if you see an item that got sold for $1000.00 with 55 bids on it, you don't need to be a rocket scientist for you to figure out that there are a lot of buyers out there looking for this item like crazy. if you find the same item and put it up for sale, may be you find it and buy it cheaper from someone who don't know what it's what because not everyone is into eBay selling, you will get the same reaction from the buyers and make a lot of profit. After Spiderman old comic book had sold for over $200,000.00, people stormed antique shops, yard sales, flea markets, craigslist, talked to friends and relatives, placed ads, did whatever they could they get this thing from people who had kept or collected those from the past and don't know what it's worth or what to do with it, and a lot of people made banks with those. I am just giving you a principle which you can take and apply to every aspect of eBay you want to sell in. Completed listing is used to find hot selling items on eBay, period. No guess works, no mistakes, no gimmicks, guaranteed to sell and make you money.

5. WRITING YOUR RULES AND POLICIES

You don't have to be a legal practitioner to write rules and policies to cover and protect you business. Your goal should be with only one thing in mind - 'to cover all possible loopholes in dealing with your buyers that will be against your business interest especially on what happens after a transaction takes place' That's all about it. You would want your customers to have that option of returning an item if for some reason after purchasing it they want it returned either for exchange or refund, which of course is not a good news for your business but it gives them the flexibility and increases their buyer confidence in you when they see you have such policy in place. However, you will make them take some responsibilities towards that too, like making it clear that buyer will pay for the return shipping and stipulating the number of days within which customers wishing to return item either for exchange or refund have to do so. In my return policy on eBay, I put a little contingency stating that customers with such intention to return the item must contact me within 3 days from the day item is delivered to be issued an MRA# (merchandise return authorization #) and have 7 business days from the delivery date to return the item for a full refund. Notice the differences in days here; 3 days to contact me and 7 business days to return the item all starting from the day item is delivered. Eventually some of them who wish to return item will end up falling short in complying with the details of the return policy as you stipulate it. It's all about fairness here, you want them to have choice and flexibility that will booster their buyer trust and confidence to buy from you, but at the same time let them understand the responsibility that goes with freedom and choice.

You can also add fees for restocking any returned item for refund, on damaged or compromised items. Be as detailed as possible and try as much not to leave any loopholes, because, believe me, a customer may not be that critical in analyzing your return policy details until he or she finds himself or herself in a situation where he or she wants the item returned. Then will they analyze your return policy from word to word, sentence to sentence, line to line and from paragraph to paragraph, trying hard to find any possible lapse that gives him/her the footing to decline the transaction. I am saying these out of my own personal experience. I learnt the hard way, but am giving you this information so you don't have to repeat my mistakes.

The last rule am giving you on drop-shipping is this:

"Never you ever do or say anything to your customers whether implicit or explicit, that will give your customer(s) the impression that you are just a middleman between them and another seller". They will feel ripped off, thus mistrust, and mistrust alone will make a lot of them give you negative feedbacks on eBay. You don't want anything to put your seller account rating in that situation. That will be really BAD! If the item is a hot selling item, which means you are selling a lot of those, you don't have to return it back to the seller if your buyer asks for refund as long as the item is not compromised in anyway that could jeopardize the re-selling or the value of the item. But if it's one of those you hardly sell, then you have to return it to your seller because you will not know it it's going to be sold again and how long it is going to take before you have a serious buyer for it. By the way, you shouldn't have any business with items like that because you suppose to have done all your research using the proving and practical guidelines I earlier on in this book explained and walked you through. If you not sure or if you already forgot, stop right now, go back and re-visit that column. One of the worst things that can happen to any business is purchasing stagnant products for sale. This will not only swallow up your capitals but drown and cripple your business as well. But it won't happen to you because this information is making you a better informed seller, not just for selling on eBay but in any other business you intending to do

6. LISTING PROCESS

So far we have considered the two most popular ways you can sell on eBay. Let's therefore look into how you can actually list those items on eBay to get them sold and make money which is the major reason you want to sell on eBay and for buying this book. Depending on your region, eBay has different domain names, like ebay.com for the United States region, ebay.uk for Britain, ebay.ca for Canadian region, ebay.china for Asian region, etc. The region you are determines the eBay domain access you will have, but they are all eBay marketplace. Although some regions may be more vibrant and active than others depending on the intensity and involvement in the region. The good thing about eBay is that you are not limited only to your regional eBay site alone, you can upgrade and register your seller account for your products to appear and sell on other eBay international sites. However, make sure you read and understand the various rules and policies that guide these other international eBay sites before selling your products on any or all of them. Before listing your item for sale, you have to know which of the groups in the auction/marketplace your product(s) falls in.

These are:

EBay Classified: This is where you list and sell all digital informational products like e-books, video courses, job offers, real estate, basically all personal products and services you offer and sell with your own value and standard. No items in this group are covered by eBay buyer protection (eBP). Buyers in this group are purchasing such products or services at their own risk. Though eBay provide sellers in this group a marketplace platform for them to sell their products and services, the transactions are never completed with eBay, they are completed outside of eBay. Personal information of sellers in this group is given to the buyers so that if interested, they can contact the sellers and complete the transaction outside of eBay. EBay classified was the former kijiji.com eBay purchased and made it part of its marketing community. However, you don't need to worry about which section or group on eBay you need to list your item because once you choose your category for your item, it will automatically put your item in its right group.

There is this other section called **eBay motors** - a section of eBay specifically designed for automotive sales and parts.

The third and probably the most used by most sellers, the most visited by most buyers is the general auction marketplace for everything else which is where you are most likely to be selling.

Every item you sell on eBay has its own category. It's how eBay group similar items or items with similar qualities and values. It is imperative you list your item with proper category or else your item will be removed or could get your eBay account restricted or even suspended. If you are a new seller on eBay, your seller account will be restricted to 10 item listings per month or USD500.00 per month, whichever comes first. However, you can always request the customer service for limit increase but you have to establish some positive sales record and good customer ratings. The longer you sell on eBay with positive buyer ratings, the more you get a limit increase. Now eBay does hot only have a limit restriction on new sellers, it also has some category restriction too for new buyers. This means that if you are a new seller, there are certain categories they may not allow you to list in until you establish positive selling record or until you have sold on eBay for at least 90 days

(3 months). These categories are determined by the dollar amount of the items listed on them, basically as a newbie, each item you list can't exceed certain dollar amount until you establish a good seller record. However, you can always call the customer representative to discuss your limit increase any time.

Once you have a total sales record of about $2000.00 or $3000.00, and again with good and positive sales record, eBay will offer you the choice of opening and owning an eBay store. There are many benefits that come with owning eBay store. Two most important of those are the fact that you now have an unrestricted selling or listing limits, you won't be concerned any more on the number of items left before you reach your selling limits for the month. The second benefit of having an eBay store is that it saves you money on all the outrageous and ridiculous eBay selling fees and that suppose to get your attention as a prospective eBay seller. For instance while others are paying $0.50 insertion fee for fixed listings, eBay store owners will be paying $0.20. This may not seem to be a lot for you but it adds up very quickly. List 50 items, fixed price style and you will be paying $25.00, while a seller with eBay store will be paying only $10.00. That's a whopping difference of $15.00. So the more of such listings the more fees you rack up. Also with eBay store comes all 12 picture uploads free. Usually only the first picture you upload to title description is free the rest of it you would want to upload will cost you $0.15 each. That's $1.65 for the remaining 11 pictures. Again the fees add up fast. Although eBay plans on reversing this policy. I think very soon all pictures will be free for all sellers regardless of their different selling levels and limits, and that's good news. This is just some of the basic benefits of owning eBay store. **There are three types of eBay store:** the **first level** is $15.00 per month, **second level** is $39.99 per month and the **third level** is mainly used by the power-sellers and costs $299.99. Each of these store types has its own benefits and individual features. For now you just need a basic seller account to get started, everything else will follow

7. OPENING MULTIPLE EBAY ACCOUNTS

Talking about seller account, you can also open a multiple eBay seller account. This means you can have more than one seller account on eBay. This is against eBay policy if you don't do it the right way. EBay expect sellers who wish to have multiple accounts to link them all together to one account. This helps eBay to access all your seller account through your central account. There is a benefit to this in the sense that when you open a new seller account, and link it to your already established account, your selling limit of the new account will receive an automatic limit increase reflecting what you have on your established account. But there is a catch. If your central account has problems in terms of low rating standard and poor seller performance, any restrictions or actions against you by eBay, will automatically affect every other account linked to it. So the best thing is to open your additional seller account separate with different emails without linking anything. You will have a selling limit for a start but the account will be totally independent. This is against eBay policy and you have to be sure there is no red flag that may trigger suspicion about you opening multiple accounts because that can get your seller account suspended on eBay. Now, though you may have multiple accounts with eBay but you don't have to open multiple pay pal accounts. I personally had similar experience before I figured out how to handle it. If you have a new account with eBay and an item is sold through that account, eBay will receive the payment and submit your information to pay pal and pay pal will open an account on your behalf, all these happen automatically. All you need to do is follow the email instructions and confirm your identity with pay pal and claim your cash. This means the more independent accounts you open with eBay, the more account you will have with pay pal because whenever any of the new account has its first sale, a new account will be automatically opened for you with pay pal with the email associated with that eBay seller account. So to avoid having multiple pay pal account I will teach you a simple strategy you will use to take care of all that.

This is how it works, when you open a new eBay seller account, during the listing of your items, on the column where you are required to enter your pay pal account with which to accept payment, delete the auto-generated email account eBay in that field, which is usually the email address associated with that seller account, and type in the email of your pay-pal account you would wish to use to collect your payments. You can use the same pay-pal email account on all your different eBay seller account listings and still elude detection from eBay for having an unlinked multiple seller account. So what this means is that though you have more than one seller account on eBay, but at the end all the sales from all these different accounts will be gathering into one pay-pal account. This helps you manage your finances well and better keep track of your sales, instead of having multiple pay-pal account and constantly logging in and out from one pay-pal account to the next. The strategy is as simple as that. I have done the investigation, the calculation and the experimentation, the strategy works and you will remain under radar undetected with your multiple accounts on eBay. However the down side is that if any of those accounts is suspended by EBay, the rest are likely to be suspended as EBay detects similarity in Pay-pal email account used with the suspended account and any other account/s. EBay uses a super-intelligent software to control and monitor all the activities of its buyers and sellers. Almost every activity on eBay is automated. This basically means that when you are selling or buying on eBay, it's you versus the computer. Therefore when any of your account is suspended indefinitely from selling or buying on eBay, the software scours automatically every account on eBay for links and similarities to the suspended account which includes but not limited to same personal names, same address, same phone number and same pay-pal transaction email account. Now you should know that software records your IP ADDRESS of your computer. For those who don't know what IP ADDRESS is, it is a unique number that identifies your computer on internet. So if your account is indefinitely suspended, you will not be able to open any new eBay account with the same computer. If you do, it will be blocked within 24 hours. So if your account is suspended by eBay, you are basically screwed.

However, there is still away out even when your account is suspended indefinitely from selling on eBay. The information am giving you here is cutting edge – meaning that about 99% of people don't know about, you're among the lucky 0.1% who know it. I have personally studied the technicalities on how the eBay software intelligence works and have come out with an amazing discovery. A lot of people have unintentionally given up to their aspirations and dreams of selling and making thousands of dollars on eBay because their accounts were suspended and all effort they make to open new ones to see if they could beat that system, failed wholly. I've been there myself. My central account was suspended because too many negative feedbacks from those customers that will never satisfied, no matter what you do to please them, they want your item and they want it almost free. Most of these customers are those who shop regularly on eBay and know how it works. They take advantage of the feedback influence they have on your account performance rating as buyers to extort you. They will ask you for an exchange or return, even after they have used this item for a good while. They will even ask you to give them some of their money back because they think the price your sell it to them is too high compared to its other kinds on eBay. When you give them the reason why it's not fair to your business to satisfy them exactly the way they wanted, they will give you negative feedbacks, and you can only have but a few of those before you start getting warnings, restrictions and suspensions on your account by eBay, and not long you will wake up one morning to see all your selling accounts indefinitely suspended. I experienced all that first hand so I know exactly what I'm talking about. So how do you beat this powerful detection software so you can still sell on eBay? Easy, just avoid all the stuff the software looks for in order to link the account to the suspended one.

This is how you do. **First**, do not register any new eBay account with the same **computer** you've been using in accessing those suspended accounts. **Second**, do not use your **personal name** again while opening any new account, however the name you use has to be a real legal name. This means you will talk to your family member or a friend to get permission to use their names and possibly their addresses too, to open an eBay account. Of course you open any new account with new email address, and you can create a lot of those from yahoo or gmail. **Third**, avoid using the same **home address** you used in any of those suspended accounts. **Fourth**, avoid using the same **phone number** you used while registering any of those suspended accounts. **Fifth**, avoid using the same **pay-pal transaction emails account** you used in any of those suspended accounts. So this means you have to use a different name, different home address, different computer for registering and accessing the new account, different contact phone number and different email address for your pay-pal transactions. Follow these five guidelines strictly well, and you will beat that software to the race. That's right, this is why my book is like no other out there when it comes to selling on eBay. I don't just teach you what to do to become a successful seller on eBay, but I also anticipated the worst case scenarios you may encounter selling on eBay and offer you a practical and technical solutions to those unlike any other. You ought to be grateful and thankful for this book.

8. CHOOSING CATEGORY

We have already touched on categories and listings earlier in this book. So you have opened an account and used the strategy I already taught you in this book to determine the niche item to sell on eBay to make a lot of money and you are ready to list the item. Your next step is to choose the category in which to list your item. The process is very simple; log into your eBay seller account, place the cursor on 'SELLING', on the drop down row, click on 'sell an item'. Item search field will appear asking you to type in description word(s) for your item. Click on search after typing in the description word(s), system will automatically suggest some categories under which the item appears. 9 out of 10 one of those categories suggested will definitely match the item you are trying to sell. Check on the box beside the category that best describe your item. You can check on more than one box, meaning that your item will appear on more than one category to potential buyers but more categories means more fees from eBay. Once you check on the box look down below there will be a link asking you to see items listed with the selected category. The reason for this is so you can see, confirm and be sure the category you choose is the right one for your item. When you click on that link, it will show you completed listings of the type of items in that category. You can see their listing format, bids, prices and what the ones that sold, sold for. It also helps you with pricing your items so you do not either over-price and scare potential customers or under-price and make potential buyers think your item is of very low quality or value. You will see your potential competition and that will help you figure out what you may do differently to dominate the competition.

Okay, at this point I am going to give you a secret, a niche in maximizing your listings and sales. **Always think outside the box** when listing your item. Let me give you an example of what am trying to say. If you have a bakery pan to sell on eBay and everyone else is listing theirs on pots and pans category. You can think of so many other ways that particular pan can be useful to people or think of some other things people can use that pan for and list it with a different category instead of the category where everyone else is listing theirs. Little tricks like this can give a seller an edge on eBay, an advantage over other sellers. Strategies like this eliminates most of the competition for you because there aren't many people to compete with since there wouldn't be that many sellers listing their pans with that category where you will be listing yours. So if you don't remember anything about choosing a category,

remember to always think outside the box in terms of figuring out some other ways that particular item could be used differently apart from generally or commonly known usage of it.

LISTING WITH EBAY CATALOGUE

EBay is continually improving and enhancing the site bringing in a lot of features to maximize seller and buyer experience, also to get a better handle on the auction marketplace activities of both buyers and sellers, and millions of items and transactions that take place on eBay daily. One of the ways eBay does this is by providing what they call 'eBay catalogue'. This is mainly for most electronic products. It's what its name suggest 'Catalogue'. This is a catalogue that contains most electronic items and devices, of course not all, but most. The catalogue contains the manufacturers' description of most electronic items. Therefore when you choose a category and it falls within the items that are listed on the catalogue, eBay requires you list your item using the catalogue description provided. The catalogue contains different brands, models, makes, and in some cases the color of some of these electronic products. Scroll and click on the one that best describes the one you are selling. The catalogue also contains specific item pictures for an easy and proper identification. When you choose your item from the catalogue and click on 'sell yours' link, the product description and picture (if available) upload automatically to your listing page. However this does not replace your personal description of the item you are selling in terms of any modification and changes in the original manufacturer condition of the merchandise. EBay still requires you to personally describe the item you are selling and take full responsibility of your sales. Item not received as described by the buyer is subject to a return from the buyer, and it doesn't matter if you have no return policy on the item. No return policy on your item can only be enforced if your description of the item matches with what the buyer sees when he or she actually buys and receives the item. If it does not, buyer has every right to send the item back to you for a full refund or exchange. We will talk about describing your item in a minute because they are all part of listing process.

However if you're required to list your item with the catalogue but the particular item is not on the catalogue, you can still list without the catalogue by clicking on 'list without the catalogue' link. You can send a message to eBay to add that item to their catalogue.

Click on the request link down below and send your request. Let's move on therefore to item description column where you will give it your personal description.

9. DESCRIBING YOUR ITEM

Whether you are a beginner - a novice, not too new to eBay selling or may be you think you have mastered the listing tricks on eBay, well, you need to pay attention to some things we are going to talk about in this section. The truth of the matter is, and you have to get this stuck at the back of your mind whenever you are listing your item on eBay for sale: **"Your item is as good as you describe it to the buyers"** and that's the one sentence that best summarizes just about anything we need to say concerning the importance of proper and excellent item description. As said earlier, even if your item is one of those listed with eBay catalogue, you still have to personally describe your item in the item description column provided. This way you are taking full responsibility for whatever item, product or merchandise you sold to anyone on eBay. So if your item is as good as you describe it to buyers, it therefore means that the better chance of your item selling well on eBay and dominating your competitors', relies a greater extent on how good your description of your merchandise is able to appeal to your potential buyers. I would want you to do a little research on eBay. Go to eBay website, pick randomly more than one seller of similar product, you will notice some sellers have more bids on the item and it got sold while some have little or no offers at all on similar item and it never got sold. This is pure statistics. So why is it so? Well lower prices, incentives or other combined offers by some sellers may play a part to it. We will discuss pricing and incentives more in upcoming chapters. However, up to 75% chance of your item being sold on eBay will be attributed to an excellent and well detailed item description.

Therefore through years of my experience selling on eBay, I have narrowed the tricks of an excellent item description down to science and brought it to books, providing methodology and systematic approach, creating guidelines and rules designed through years of proven results, to give your item description such thumbs up as to appeal and influence your potential buyers. So what are these requirements for an excellent eye-catching description? If you have not really paid attention to everything we've said so far on listing your item, you really do need to pay attention to this one. This is where you will give your item the voice it so desperately need to be able to speak to all your potential buyers, get their attention and most likely influence their decision and convince them to make a purchase or bid on your item. Now some already popular items do not need much of description. Products like i-pads and similar items that already have worldwide brand name reputation and are always in demand. This does not mean that you won't describe the item in your own words in the description column, of course, you will, but just don't have to do too much so as to convince your potential buyers since these products already speak for themselves because of their popularity, reputation and continually increasing consumer demand. One of the reasons why you still have to describe the item is so you can take full responsibility for whatever merchandise you are selling on eBay. If a customer buys an item and it does not match or lack in any of the descriptions you give it on your listing page on eBay, the buyer is entitled to return the item for an exchange or a full refund (purchase price + shipping cost paid). Nice customers can do that without reporting you to eBay, which of course, as you may know is an eBay policy violation. However, some will not only report you to eBay but give you negative feedbacks. The flaws in your description may be a mistake or unintended oversight but some customers may not be willing to give you any benefit of doubt, and you can understand that. Just put yourself in their position: You need a product, you find one on eBay, the description you read of it get you so excited that you actually go ahead and purchase the item, only to receive it and the actual product lacks in all or some of the descriptions the seller gives it on eBay that gets you all worked up and excited to wanting to buy the item. You wouldn't like that, or would you? So you understand why eBay have that policy in place and why you shouldn't do such to your buyers, not even oversights or mistakes of such is acceptable or excusable.

Make sure your description covers the physical and the overall condition of the item you are selling such as blemishes, wears, tears, etc. Anything short of the manufacturers' original condition of the item has to be described in this section so the buyer knows exactly what he or she is buying. When the customer physically receives the item, it has to match as described in your description in that item listing on eBay. I can't say this enough, and I will say it again, if the buyer receives the item and it does not exactly match as described on eBay or lacks in certain quality as described, the buyer has every right to return the item to you, it doesn't matter what your return policy says. This is a violation of eBay policy and your account can be suspended as a result. Secondly, it's taken to be an intentional deception of buyers to trick them into buying your product willingly knowing that it doesn't fit all the description or lacks in some of the descriptions you give to it in your listings, that you use false, incorrect or incomplete information about your item to deceive potential customers to buying it. Same goes with positive qualities of your item. Customers want to know all the good qualities and all the use of the products, especially basic use, in the description page. This is to your advantage because by doing so, you are giving your item a voice to make positive impact on the customers which will definitely influence their decision whether to buy your product or not. Remember this: **"The best principle to follow while describing your item is to place yourself in the position of a buyer."** After describing your item, go and look at a few other descriptions from already sold items like yours from the **'completed listings'**. Then ask yourself if you are a buyer, which of these descriptions including yours best motivate and influence your decision to buy this particular item. There is no other way you can get around the answer to this question because the truth will be staring you at the face. If it's yours that you choose, well congratulations, you've done it, but if it's other sellers', well find out the things about that description that make it get so much attention and able to get you interested more than your own ad. Extract that description trick or tricks you identify on that listing and use it to format yours. Remember it's illegal to copy someone's ideas verbatim, word to word, sentence to sentence, line to line and place it in your own description. It's called **plagiarism** and that can get you in trouble if the original generator of those ideas finds out and decides to pursue it. If you use any material that does not originate from you in your listing and the owner happens to find out and reports to eBay, they will cancel all such related listings you have and make you take a quiz meant to educate you on such issues before you can gain access to list any items with that account again. But you can apply the same principle, format or guidelines the person followed in your own unique way, words and style without violating any copyrights or committing plagiarism.

Always remember to describe your item 'as is' without hiding or with-holding anything on both the physical and overall condition of the item whether on the things it lacks or the positive values including the usage. Put yourself in the position of the potential buyer and see if your listing has what it takes to motivate and influence your decision to buy the product. Write proper title and choose the correct item condition. Those fields of course, are mandatory. The item condition field has New, Used, Refurbished, etc options. Choose whichever best describe the condition of the merchandise you are selling, and please be honest. If you are honest with your buyers and the item you sold them is as described on your listings, you can always expect positive feedbacks from your buyers because what they get is what they buy and what they buy is exactly what the see. These positive feedbacks matter a lot if you are to make a good living selling on eBay because eBay use those to rate your standing as a seller and your scores go a long way to qualifying you in being able to receive all the free offers and incentives eBay gives to the sellers every now and then; from free listings to subsidized listing fees. Every month, eBay computes sellers' ratings from their monthly performance which combines both policy compliance and seller feedbacks to determine whether a seller performance rating is below eBay standard, meets the standard or exceeds the standard. If it's below, you will automatically be excluded from some of the offers and incentives, but if it meets the standard or exceeds it, you are in. Do not forget that words go around because people will always spread the word. If you have a great product and treat your buyers right, they will always share their experience with others and thereby directly or indirectly referring them to buy from you. It's in our human nature to always look for closer friends and pals to share our excitement with. This will definitely increase your sales in no time.

Anyway, don't be sidetracked yet, though the information we shared above is a necessary diversion. We are still talking about describing your item, the best way to do it to catch the attention of potential buyers, the kind description that holds the stop sign on eBay buyers and get them to pause for a minute whenever they land on you description page.

10. THE USE OF GRAPHICS

Understanding the psychology of online shoppers - As true with eBay, same is true with every other online shopping or marketing site. You have to know that online shopping is a lot different from offline shopping where you physically walk into and through the store, and evaluate the item using your 5 senses of sight, touch, smell, hearing and sometimes taste. When you physically walk into the store for shopping you have a lot of tools at your disposal to help you make an informed decision. However, in online shopping the experience is different since there aren't a lot of tools to examine the item as you normally would in an offline shopping situation. The only powerful tool of evaluation available to an online shopper is his or her sense of sight, sometimes hearing, with good sound effects. If you as an online marketer or eBay seller can get this info tip in your mind, it will change your selling strategy for good, because it will help you understand the importance of the use of graphics in your online advertisement and item description on eBay. Your eBay shopper online shoppers cannot physically touch or feel, smell or feel the item you're selling them. They can only see it which means the better the visual appeal the more the chances of them buying the item. The clear and intelligent description you give your item help them in judging and evaluating in terms of their reasons for wanting to buy the item. The use of excellent graphics brings in persuasion and appeal.

You may have a not-so-wonderful written item description, but excellent graphics of the item will not only tell the shoppers all the need to know but also gives the appeal and persuasion that influences their decision to purchase that product. Why? Because online customers shop with their eyes only and it's all about visual appeal. Therefore, if you as an online seller can grasp, understand and permanently internalize this simple psychology of online selling and online buyers, and make it your guide when listing and describing your merchandise on eBay, you will be able to beat the hundreds and thousands of your competitors on eBay. Unless the item you are selling is so unique and rare, the truth is that there are hundreds, if not thousands of people selling similar product on same eBay auction site.

There are 2 types of graphics you can use in describing your item: The **video** graphics and the **pictorial** graphics. You can use either one of those or combine both for a powerful and outstanding description of your item. However given the choice, I'll choose the video graphics.

Video graphics is when you make short video clips ranging from a few seconds to up to 10 minutes long but don't make it too long, just short video clip packed with information about the item that will leave your potential buyers wanting to see and no more, use the persuasive appeal of the clip to create and element of suspense in your customers. Visual description is proven to be so effective, because, not only that the potential buyer get to see the motion pictures about the item, they'll also get to watch the visual demonstration of how to use the item. They will see how the item is being assembled, installed, used, applied, and basically the outlined, simple and short steps from installation to usage. It gets them involved and excited, addressing possible issues some customers initially feared or anticipated. Your short clip can be a short intro, a quick start guide and usage of the product or how it actually works. Even if you don't have anything on your item description page, an embedded short clip only can take care of your entire description but be sure the video shows every possible defects on the item and addresses any issues with the product especially if the products you selling is a used item or and antique. This is very important because if the description you give to your item in you description does not match the actual product the buyer received, the buyer has every right to return the product to you for a full refund, and it's a serious violation of eBay policy which can get your account restricted or suspended. Remember, you are responsible for any items you sell to your customers.

HOW DO YOU CREATE AND EMBED THE VIDEO?

A lot of newer gadgets and hand-held devices come with built-in front and rear-view cameras that allow you to record your activities or videotape yourself without the assistance of anyone. A lot of phone sets have dual (front and rear) cameras. Same with a lot modern day laptops and notebook computers including tablet PCs, I-pads, etc. Now there are many tools you can utilize and a lot of sites you can use to upload your video clips online but my all time favorite and the most commonly used is the world's largest video sharing community - 'The Youtube' - youtube.com. Most of these gadgets come with youtube application already installed in them ready for use. Of course you know youtube is now owned and managed by the famous Google Company. Some digital cameras with internet access also have youtube application in them. Just make your video and upload it on youtube but first you have to have a youtube account which is very simple and easy to set up in one minute or less, just follow the instructions and the steps. Once your account is confirmed, you can upload your video to your youtube account. However, this is not the end, remember your goal is to embed the video on your eBay item listings description page. EBay has disabled live video features on description page, but I will still go ahead and teach you how to do it should in case they decide in the future to enable that feature, you won't be lost. This book will still serve as your guide.

So how do you copy and paste this video link from youtube to eBay? Easy! Simply look for the link on the home page of that particular youtube that says 'share this video' and click on it. When you click on it, a field will appear with highlighted link. Place the cursor on the highlighted link and right-click, on the options menu window that will appear when you right-click the highlighted link, select and right click on 'copy'. That's it. You've just copied that video clip youtube link. Now go to your eBay page, on that particular item's description column because that's where you will be embedding the link of the youtube video you've just copied on youtube.

At the top of the eBay item description column, there will be two clickable fields, depending on the way you want to describe your item. The first says 'standard' and the second 'HTML' - abbreviation for Hotmail. Standard field is for regular standard typing, copying and pasting. The description field is already set on standard, so you don't need to click on it whenever you get to that column to describe your item. However, you are not supposed to paste the video link you copied from youtube on the standard field in your description column. If you do, the clip will never come to live after you publish your listing on eBay, it will never play. So this is where the HTML comes in. Whenever you are ready to embed your video in the description click on the html field. If you already have something written in standard description format, when you click on the html, all the inscriptions will appear in bunch of incomprehensible codes and symbols that practically do not make any sense but that's the way all your entries are coded and interpreted in the system. It's like the non-digital camera film negatives. When you look at those film negatives, you can hardly tell whose image those are but once it is developed, everything about the image becomes very clear with viewing definition. Then you will be able to tell what or whose image they are.

After you clicked on the html and the description column has switched to html field which is easily recognized because all the entries you already have in your description will turn into codes and symbols. Place and left-click on the cursor at the spot where you want the video embedded. Right-click on the cursor, in the options field that will appear, scroll down and left-click on 'paste'. The video link you previously copied from youtube will be embedded at that particular spot. Now there may be a little confusion trying to identify the particular spot this video clip link will paste in the html field to look proper and right when changed in the standard field. But if you want to do it randomly then you wouldn't babe any problems, you simply click and embed at any desired spot. There is a trick I will show you on how you can identify the exact spot you intend to embed the video when on html field. For instance in standard field, this reads: **'selling on eBay is co-o-o-ol'**. However if you click on the html, the same text will display like this: **' a#bc.#a<a>aqlp><#ebk'** in html field. So tell me, if you intend to embed your video link between **'is'** and **'co-o-o-ol'** in html field, and everything looks as written above in html field, how would you identify in the midst of all these mixed up codes and symbols, the exact spot you intend to embed the video? This is what you do; in-between the 'so' and 'co-o-o-ol' click and type in the letter **'x'** preferably, could be any letter of your choice, up to **6 Xs** in the standard text. When you click on the html look closely and see where among those codes and symbols, delete those and paste your video link in that spot. This exactly is the secret on how to identify the spot where you need the video embedded. After pasting the link on the html field, click on the 'standard' option to view the video in the regular standard format.

11. PICTORAL GRAPHICS

As the name suggest, this is simply the use of images in describing your merchandise. To do this you need a digital camera with at least 3 mega-pixels or more with clear background. Depending on the item, your pictures should cover front, back, sideways, up and under. Be sure to eliminate any distortion that may blur the image or give a false representation of a specific point of interest. There are two places pictures are seriously needed when listing your item. First is the picture upload column. This is where you upload pictures that are to be shown with your item's listing title on eBay auction. The first picture you upload is free depending on the category you are listing in and also on your subscription level too. For example if you have an eBay store, all 12 pictures you upload are free. Sometimes listing with certain categories gives you free which means you can upload up to the maximum number of pictures allowed - 12 packs, categories like collectibles and antiques. But if none of this applies to you or to any of your listing categories, the first picture you upload is free and 15¢ for any additional. However you really don't have to upload up to 12 pictures of your item in your listing, in most cases, one clear picture is enough to get the message across. A good picture to associate the title with an image to get to get more attention and better traffic to your listing. Picture(s) should be targeted. Be sure the picture you are uploading displays any possible particular point of interest customers most likely to get excited about viewing the picture image of the item.

Now your description column should have pictures of your item to help customers stay focused on the image of your item. This is one of the major mistakes a lot of not-well-informed seller make. They upload few pictures to go with item's title but have no pictures of the item on the description column. Photos in description field are not uploaded, they're just normal copy and paste. Google image search will display the pictures of about anything. Simply type in your item name or phrase or related keywords in Google search and click enter. When the page is completely displayed, look at the left side of the window and click on image. Google search engine will display all the images related to your search word. Scroll down and find image or images that best describe what you want. Place the computer cursor on the image, right-click and then select copy. Click on any place you want the pictures to appear on your description column, left-click first then right-click, select and click on 'paste'.

The text or image will be pasted in the space. Please be careful and very mindful of plagiarism when using any material that does not originate from you. Do your due diligence before using any material you found on the internet.

There are few words you would have to avoid using completely on the description field if you want the system to accept your listing. Words like: power-seller, super-seller, top-rated, top-seller, phone numbers or sets of numbers that might trigger any suspicions that suggest telephone numbers, websites, etc. You have to understand that when you are selling on eBay, it's you versus the system computer. The entire marketplace has been pre-programmed and pre-fed with eBay rules, policies and guidelines. Whenever the software detects violation from a seller it automatically sends out a reminder, warning notice, limitation or restriction notice, suspension or even account termination depending on the level of your violations. Please note that if your seller account is suspended or terminated on eBay, this does not mean you cannot access your account any more. Of course you will still access your account and perform administrative actions, you just can't do any more listings with that account until the issues with it is resolved. It is also your responsibility to complete all pending transactions you have with anyone customer or buyer and maintain communication with them until such time that it's not necessary any more as stipulated by your policy.

Sometimes when eBay send you an email notice because of a violation, placing a temporary restriction on your account and asking that you call customer service to resolve the issue, I personally suggest that you don't call any customer service. You probably may not understand why, but I will explain with a personal experience selling on eBay for years. Take this as a warning. If the restriction is mild and temporary just for a couple of days, I suggest you do not call any customer representative to help you resolve the matters with your account because if you do, they will use that opportunity to review your entire eBay account activities thoroughly and will cross examine you to access your level of understanding and knowledge of eBay seller rules, policies and practice, at the end of which they are more likely to put a much stricter limits or restrictions on your account or even suspend it. Secondly, depending on the outcome of the examination, they may place your account under radar for close monitoring. So if the limitation or restriction is not extreme or permanent as generated automatically by the system, do not contact customer representative.

Try also to avoid negative feedbacks as much as you can from your buyers. Negative feedback is the easiest and fastest way to lower your seller rating. The system reviews seller accounts every 20 days. If you have any problems with your buyer, try resolving it as much as possible and increase communication with your buyers. Most problems sellers have with buyers are due to lack of proper communication. If a customer purchases an item and for some reason you can't ship as promised, write the buyer and let him know the item or a part to it is out of stock at the moment. Apologize for the oversight and ask if he or she want to wait for it, want a partial shipping and then ship the remaining part later or simply want a full refund. Nine times out of ten most customers understand, and am telling you this out of my personal experience as an established eBay seller. I had a similar situation, a messy one indeed but I got smart and creative about it. I communicated with my buyers, humbly explained the situation to them with some apologies of course and offered them possible choices. This was the situation: I sold a lot of my items to a lot of customers but it happened that part of the item was out of my stock and to make matters worst, I don't even have enough cash on hand to place the order. Now all those payment I received from my customers was not yet available on pay-pal because of pay-pal policy in which they put a hold on your funds until they automatically confirm, through electronic shipping tracking that the item has been delivered. Pay-pal will automatically release your funds 3 days after delivery is electronically confirmed and the recipient never complained.

So what I did was to email and explained the situation to all my buyers that I have their items but a piece to it was out of stock without my knowledge. I suggested a few options to them. Of course it was only one email message I composed that I duplicated and sent to each buyer. I asked them if they want a partial shipping whereby I will ship what I have available and will ship the remaining when my stock comes in a few days time or if they would want to wait for the stock to arrive so I could send the whole thing all at once or if they want a full refund of their payment back. 98% of them agreed to the suggestion of partial shipping, and that was exactly what I did. I shipped the items with tracking info. Items were delivered, pay-pal tracked the delivery and three days after, most of the fund was available for me which I used to place the orders with faster shipping service.

As soon as those arrived, I mailed them out to those buyers concerned. But the key here is timely communication with your buyers and keeping them updated with the situation. As far as feedback is concerned, you can write your previous buyers who had completed transaction with you but never left feedback and encourage them to do so, be sure to leave a positive feedback for the first so that may motivate them to leave one for you.

You need to understand that eBay has no problem suspending your seller account, it does not matter if you are a power seller with thousands of positive feedbacks from your customers. If your account indulges in any serious eBay policy violations, the system will automatically restrict your account privileges or even suspend it as the case may be. Remember what we said earlier about how you can't use certain words with your item description field. However, there are smart ways you can do that and stay undetected. Take for instance you want to insert your personal business web address so you can drive eBay buyer traffic to your personal webpage. The system won't allow you to do that. EBay as you already know is known for its high quality buyer traffic and if there are some creative ways you can use to channel some of that traffic to your independent website, that will be fine. So how can you do that without being detected and remain below the radar? Here's the trick on how to do that. For instance, if you want to display your store name or your web address information on your listing do that with the pictures you will upload with your listings; the title description pictures and in your item description page. There are so many and different gadgets available for you to do this. Touch-screen digital camera is my first choice, the ones that have the features which allow you to modify the pictures you take and save the changes.

These digital cameras allow you to write anything on the pictures and save to become part of the picture. So take the picture of your item with one of these digital cameras and depending on the feature menu, touch on edit and follow and features and write the name of your business or website or whatever is it you want to write on the picture, then save it. Therefore when you upload that same picture on either your title description column or item description field the picture of the item will be showing with your business infomercial. That is how you manipulate that and get around the strict eBay rules. However, there is another, a less technical way you can do it if you do not have one of those digital cameras or may be, you're not all that tech-inclined. Take the pictures of the item, print them out, then use a color bright marker that can cancel the background color of the picture and write the info you wanted on the pictures, then take another picture of the picture with the info written on it and upload to your listing. So these are just few ways you can display your personal info on your listings without being detected. SMART!!! Huh!!! Nonetheless, keep your fingers crossed and pray that none of your competitors does not recognize and report your account to eBay. Some sellers do that just to eliminate as many competitions as they possibly can. If you become a victim of such, please do not take it personal.

12. AUCTION BIDS

Understanding and creating bids: When you put up an item for auction sale with a starting price whereby interested buyers who wish to purchase the item keep adding to it, sometimes at a set increment amount until either the reserve price is met and/or it's sold to the highest bidder, this is what auction is all about and the process is called bidding. Creating bids on eBay is pretty simple. You can sell your item in two ways; either through **fixed pricing** or in **auction format**. When you sell with fixed price format, you do not allow the potential buyers to bid on the item. There's a **fixed price** on the item and whoever is interested can buy it at that price. You can also choose to accept offers from interested buyers. If you choose that option in you fixed price listing, the system will display the price of your item with the message: 'Buy It Now Or Best Offer'. This means the seller of this item will be willing to consider reasonable offers. However, if you click on auction format, it allows you to create a bidding process for your item starting with any price of your choice anywhere from 1¢ and up. Most bidding processes start at 99¢. Now you need to understand the psychology of the bidding process.

When you start your auction bid with a very low and insignificant bid amount, it attracts a lot of bidders, and an item that has a lot of bidders stands the better chance of being sold among the many others of kind. This is because buyers will think there is something special about that item or about the seller that make it attract such number of bidders. May be the seller or the item is more authentic than the rest of their kind on eBay, and this is exactly where you want to be in the eyes and minds of your potential buyers. Another thing is that when you start with low bidding price you will be charged low insertion fee, very low indeed because the price you list your item with determines the amount of insertion fee you will be charged, anywhere from 1¢ to $2 per item. $2 is the maximum insertion fee you will be charged no matter how big your auction listing price is. Fixed price format has its own insertion fee amount which start with 50¢ no matter how small your fixed item price is. However if you are an eligible eBay store owner and you own one, you pay 20¢ for your fixed price listing insertion. We will talk more about fees and pricing later because you need to understand how those work and how to utilize the listing features to avoid attracting too many fees so you can save your money. Now back to auction format listing, you can also add a **'Buy It Now'** price to your it. This feature basically allows buyers who don't want to go through the bidding process or to wait till the end of the auction to have the flexibility and the access to purchase the item if they wish to. Now the 'Buy It Now' feature is not free, it has a fee. However it may be free for a seller if he or she is using the 50 free auction style listings eBay gives to its sellers each month or similar incentives they give to seller from time to time. You have to be a seller in good standing as rated through your seller performance to be eligible for those free offers but if you're not, the system will charge you all applicable regular charges. This is why you need to take your good selling practices very seriously, write good item descriptions offer free shipping sometimes, ship items faster, make your buyers feel special and satisfied, these will encourage them to give you positive feedbacks, and there is nothing that improves your seller rating like positive feedbacks from your customers.

Now if you are selling with drop-shipping on eBay, I wouldn't advice you to start your auction bidding process with 99¢ because higher selling price is not always guaranteed in auction. So in order for you not to loose out on your money, if you are drop-shipping, your starting bidding price should be - the original price of the item from your seller + your own substantial profit on the item - that will be your starting bidding amount. I need to explain this a little clearer so you do not get caught up in that mistake. Take for instance you are selling on eBay with drop-shipping, if your supplier sells the item to you for $35 and you wish to put that item for auction bidding on eBay, it will be to your best interest not to start the bidding process with anything less than the original cost price of the item, in this case, $35. But the best way to do it is to add your own substantial profit to the original cost of the item, say $10, add that $35, that gives you $45. Therefore $45 becomes your starting bid. You may not have a lot of bids depending on the item you are selling but the point is that no matter the number of bids you may have on it and no matter what it's sold, the cost price and some substantial profit is already covered. I am simply expanding your mind and thinking here and giving you the principles to eBay selling success, it's up to you to take it, modify and use it in the way it best serves your interest to bring you success. Be inventive, creative and always think outside the box.

13. ACCEPTING BIDS

ACCEPTING BIDS: After you create your auction listings, the starting bid price displays in red. It turns green once an interested buyer places a bid on it by adding and increasing the bid amount. You do not have to wait till the duration of auction for the item to sell. If you feel the current bid amount is good enough for you, you can end the bid to the favor of the current higher bidder. Simply click on the options link to the right and the instructions to end the bidding and send invoice of the sale to the and send invoice of the sale to the highest bidder who of course is your winning bidder. As you do this, every other bid will be canceled and the bidders concerned automatically notified. Now if for some reason the winning bidder fails to complete the transaction, meaning, if he or she fails to make a payment and you have done all you can in terms of communication to get the customer to pay but to no avail, you can offer that same item to the second highest bidder if the bid amount is okay for you. Basically eBay is going to send them a message that the particular item they bid on is now available for them to buy it now at the final price they previously bid on the item. It's up to the buyer to accept the offer or not. You will have to choose the number of days you would want the offer to be active after which it will be canceled. If the buyer accept your offer and buys the item, eBay will charge you the final value fee which is about 9% of the selling price and on the shipping too.

This final value fee is charged once an item is sold whether you received an instant payment, get paid later and even when the buyer who won the item refuses to pay.

However there are ways and things you can do to get those final value fees credited back to your account. When you sell an item but the buyer for some reason refuses to pay, click on the actions options button at the extreme right, select and click on resolve a problem, that will take you to the resolution center click to check on the box beside the option that says: 'I **sold an item and haven't received my payment.**' If that's the only item with that non-paid item status, it will automatically display but if you have more than one sold item not yet paid for by the winning bidder, it will display all for you to make a selection. Simply check the box beside the one you wish to report and confirm it in the next page. Unpaid item case will be opened against that buyer with a notification about the action taken sent to the buyer question. Now the buyer still have four days from the day **'unpaid item case'** is opened to make payment on the item. If he or she does, the case automatically closes; eBay will still retain the final value fees. However if payment is not received within four days on the item, you can close the case by clicking on the case, then click on **'take action'** and follow the easy step by step instructions to close the case. You will automatically receive your final value fee back and an 'unpaid item case' recorded against the buyer's account. An unpaid item case can only be opened against a buyer from the 4th day after buyer has won the item and never pays.

However, like I said earlier, try to communicate with the buyer as a courtesy reminder to send in their payment but when candid communication fails, then you may open up the unpaid item case against the transaction not necessarily to record negative feedback against the buyer's account but more so you can receive the final value fees eBay will automatically charge your account whenever any of your items sells whether paid or not paid for by the buyer. Similar thing goes with canceling a transaction. You want to get back from eBay as many fees as possible whenever you have the opportunity to do so. Therefore, whenever you sell an item and the buyer end up returning the item back to you for a full refund or to want the transaction canceled, be sure to get your final value back. If a buyer makes an eligible return of an item, this means the customer complies with your return policy in terms of time, date and condition, go to the same resolution center and choose the option which says: 'I sold an item and want to cancel the transaction'. When you do that eBay will automatically send email message to the buyer in question to confirm he or she is aware of the cancellation and that he has received all applicable refund back if any. If your buyer agrees and confirms the message, the cancellation will be approved by eBay and you will receive final value fee credit on that item. The buyer has seven days to respond to the message eBay sends him or her for the cancellation. If after 7 days the buyer never acted on the message, on the 8th day you can close the case and receive your final value fee back.

AUCTION DURATION: This is basically the number of days you want your listing to remain active on eBay for potential customers or buyers to see it. This ranges from

1 day minimum to 10 days maximum. There is also thirty-day duration and the one that runs indefinite till the item is sold or you choose to end it. If you list from one to 7 auction duration days with your 50 free monthly listings or similar, you will not be charged any insertion fee or 'buy it now' option fee if you choose to use it. However, anything pass 7 days will incur you some fees. Therefore you do not need that long and extended duration. If your item can't be sold within 7 auction days, ten days may not get it sold either. It's unnecessary raking up those fees, follow the steps and guidelines I gave for killer listing description of your item and get it sold in less than 7 days. When eBay gives free listing incentives you won't be charged any insertion fees if your auction runs somewhere between 1 to 7 days. You will incur some insertion fees should you choose to run your auction for eight days or more. But just like I advised earlier, all you need is a killer listing description following the guidelines I gave earlier and your item will sell fast in less than 7days. Sometimes an item may be re-listed once or twice before it got sold. If it still does not sell, you may want to change categories and try to think outside the box, switch things around a little bit. Since buyers love free shipping, you may want to increase your price a little bit and then offer free shipping. Please understand that eBay is an extremely competitive marketplace. Each seller determines what to sale and how he or she wants to sale it.

14. BEATING THE COMPETITION

There are the so called eBay top-rated sellers or super-sellers. These are ones who have tens and hundreds of thousands of seller feedback displayed next to their seller username. Most of these people are the manufacturers, suppliers or wholesalers selling out of China. These are basically the same people you buy from at wholesale price and sell at retail price. They are potential problems for retail sellers because they are selling these items at wholesale prices on eBay, the same price they sell it to you. This is why you see same items on eBay, one sells cheap while other sells three times more. As a retail seller you have to add your own profit before selling the item. If you purchase the item at the wholesale price of $30.00 and selling it for $65.00 on eBay which includes you profit and listing fees, these top-rated sellers will be selling it for $29.99 with free shipping. So how do you plan to compete with sellers like that, sell cheaper than they do? Of course not, you will be an idiot to think that way because you will loose every dime you have.

What you have to know is that even at that ridiculously low prices they are selling these items, they still rake up a lot of profit from buyers because they get those items for even much less. This is one of the areas where creativity and thinking outside the box is extremely important and will make all the difference especially in targeting local buyers in your regional local eBay market. I had the same problem too. I will tell you how I handled it and hopefully that will explain and give you an idea on how to handle such situations in a smart way. EBay is still one of my sources of income today, I don't plan on quitting any time sooner, the money making potentials on eBay is just too big to ignore. I had a niche product idea once, which is basically taking already existing products and put them together in a way that it will offer more value to the consumers after evaluating real needs of the items in the real world. When I put this up on eBay the way I managed to put it together, it started selling like crazy.

However, its fifteen minutes of fame lasted but a few days, before the so called top-rated sellers got a hold on that product idea by searching completed listings put it together the same way I did and sold it for pennies on a dollar, three times cheaper than what I sell those. You will know when this happens because your sales will come to an almost immediate halt. The best way to figure out what is happening is to use the completed listing search criteria as we already explained earlier to view who is selling the same item and the price. When this happened, I knew I have to find another creative way to sell this product regardless. Therefore, I target my local eBay buyers and that made me come up a message I write at the top of my description column before describing the item. The message basically says that I am USA seller, home and local.

The second part of it warns local buyers on falling for the cheap price trap most oversea sellers use to get them stuck with damaged items. Now the way eBay return policy works is the if you don't like an item you purchased for some reason, you have a 14 day window of opportunity to return it back to the owner for either an exchange or for a full refund. So if you purchase an item from one of these top-rated oversea sellers for pennies on a dollar and finds out it does not work the way it should or it malfunctions and you wish to send it back for either refund or exchange, you will find out that the cost of return shipping back to the oversea seller with tracking service of course, will cost you three times more than the original cost of the item itself. So what is likely going to happen is that you will abandon the return to save your money, and of course when there are no returns, there will be no refunds or exchanges.

Therefore you are stuck with the item and the seller has no responsibilities on you unless the item is returned, you loose the item, you loose your money - double loss. I make a little comment about this to give potential buyers to my listing the reason to strongly consider buying local instead of international because of the confidence, convenience and flexibility local transactions can offer them which if translate to money worth all the price difference.

I also use priority shipping service - 2 to3 day delivery. This little comment I insert in my description surprisingly gave me my sales back and I started selling this item again despite the price tag I put on it. I simply utilized a psychological tool many sellers never thought of to create doubts in the minds of potential buyers about buying internationally and it worked. I may have lost some of my international buyers but at the same time, there is some sort of honesty in that comment that attracted me some more international buyers. Now there is not going to be any competition with any oversea top-rated seller as far as this description is concerned. Most of them are copycats, but they can't copy this one because it's a clear disadvantage they have beyond any ridiculously cheap price competition. I just give you my a one million dollar eBay sales secret because am writing this book for you to read it, apply it and succeed financially, therefore there is not need withholding any valuable information that will bring you success. So in choosing your auction duration, it's not necessarily the number of days you choose that will get your items sold but the content of your items description, the creativity and how you think outside the box to make your listings stand out in confidence and conviction to boost potential buyers enthusiasm, interest and trust to buy from you instead of the thousands of other sellers competing to sell them similar items way cheaper than you are offering in terms of pricing. The law of average does not necessarily work here which basically suggest that the longer you expose your item on auction, the more potential buyers see it and the more it's likely to be sold. If you do it the right way following the suggestions I give you in this book, the item will sell within a couple of days after listing, 5 days or less. You may also visit the completed listings, see the type of descriptions similar selling items have and use that as your description blueprint, don't copy verbatim what others wrote in their description, rather use the guidelines to create yours.

15. BUILDING YOUR SELLER REPUTATION

Now it's important you understand that as a newly registered member seller, no matter how good your item is, a lot of buyers will be hesitant to purchase from you, they would view your item but may not buy since many see you as a potential risk. EBay displays the usernames of newly registered members with little lit yellow symbols. That's how you know newly registered members. Even if you are not a newly registered member but you don't have up to 10 feedback scores, most buyers and seller will consider your status as a substantial risk when considering buying from you or not. Some buyers will click and read these feedback scores to understand the kind of reaction your previous buyers had with their transaction with you before deciding to buy from you. This is why it's always good to strive for positive feedbacks.

However don't do like most sellers do who would rather loose money so they can have a positive feedback. They are stuck with the psychology of acquiring too many feedbacks even when it's detrimental to their business profit. Do the proper thing you need to do, like when listing your item, be sure to describe it properly in your description and if it sells, be sure to ship according to your shipping policy, refund or exchange according to your return policy as clearly stipulated. That's it. Some buyers do not leave feedbacks, you can write them to remind them or simply leave them a positive feedback and they will leave you one. The thing is that once they leave you positive feedback, your fund will automatically be available for your use with pay-pal, for new sellers who have holds on their funds with pay-pal which they do to ensure trust, confidence and security for buyers and to make sure non-established sellers fulfill their part of obligation in the transaction.

16. ENDING AUCTION EARLIER AND CANCELLING BIDS

Again, this is one of the things I learnt through the hard way. Assuming you have an item listed for auction and for some reason the item is no more available for sale. This means you have to cancel all bids on the item and end the auction. If you find yourself in this situation and have no choice but to cancel, it has to be done before 12 hours to the end of the auction. Once it's 12 hours or less to the end of the auction, you won't be able to end the auction again. If the reserve price is met, you won't be able to cancel the bids or make any changes on your listing, you can add a note to your listing but won't be able to change any already existing information before the bids. When your auction has a *'Buy It Now'* price displayed with it, that starting bid is known as the 'reserve price' and once an interested potential buyer bids on it, you won't be able to cancel that bid again unless you contact the bidder and request he/she cancels or withdraws the bid. It's only the bidder he could cancel this bid by withdrawing the bid.

But if your auction does not have the *'Buy It Now'* price to it, it's an open-ended auction. You have the right and authority of access to cancel every bid on the item and end the auction itself as long as you do that before 12 hours or less to the end of the auction. However, even if it's 12 hours or less to the end of your auction, you can still cancel the bids on an open-ended auction, however, you will not be able to end the auction because it's 12 hours or less. The open-ended auction gives you more flexibility than the auction with the 'Buy It Now' option. You can't cancel any bid on this one, end the auction or be able to change any information on your listing. But with the open-ended auction, you can cancel all the bids on it at any time and be able to make any changes on your original listing information or details. Whenever a bid is cancelled, eBay automatically sends message to the bidder/s to notify them of the cancellation. To cancel bids and end auction, just click on 'cancel bids' link and carefully follow the instructions as the system walks you through the steps.

Now what happens when you sell an item but the buyer never pays? Believe me, it happens all the time. It's very important you understand that as soon as the item is sold, eBay will automatically calculate and charge you 9% final value fee on the totally sold amount, including on the shipping paid on it, and add that to the long list of your already existing eBay fees they will eventually invoice you to pay them at the end of your monthly billing period. The value fee they charge you may be more or less depending on your category and format. You have to get your final value fee back from eBay if the buyer refuses to pay so you won't be paying to eBay on item you never received a payment for. If after contacting the buyer to make payment and 4 days pass without any positive response from the buyer, click on the 'action' button to the right beside that listing and select 'report buyer' and then select 'unpaid item'. This will automatically open an unpaid item case against them and the system will automatically notify them through a sent message of the 'unpaid item case' opened against them and they have 4 days to respond, basically to pay up or resolve the issues with the seller. If after the set number of days elapses and the buyer never resolve the issues with you, go to 'resolution center' click on the 'action' button on the case, follow the steps and prompts to end and close the case. When this happens, you'll automatically be refunded on the final value fee initially charged on that item and the case is closed with an unpaid item case recorded against that buyer's account.

You follow the same steps when a buyer who purchased and paid for your item wishes to return your item for a refund per your return policy or on a qualifying return –

item may not meet your return policy but somehow short in the description you gave it in your listing. In this case you will refund the buyer as soon as the item is returned, and then follow the protocol and cancel the transaction to receive the final value fee, it's the same step. When you receive the item and send the buyer a full refund, eBay does not automatically refund you the final value fee they charge you on that item when it was sold, you have to personally initiate the refund request process for it to happen. This is the situation where you have to work with the buyer, or, may be you sold and item and wish to cancel the transaction either because you're out of stock or for whatever reason, it's the same step.

Again, once you receive the item and send the buyer a full refund, go to resolution center and open a 'cancel transaction' case, the system will walk you through. A canceled transaction case will be opened and message sent to the buyer by the system requesting him to 'confirm' or 'decline' the cancel transaction request. This is why I said earlier that you need to work together with the buyer here through decent and cordial communication. If he accepts and confirms the request, the transaction will be canceled and you will receive the final value fee back on that item. If he refuses and declines the request, you will not receive any final value back. Oh! Talking about fees, let's look at the different fees you pay to list and sell an item on eBay.

17. UNDERSTANDING MOST EBAY SELLER FEES

Final Value Fee: If there is one thing that can demoralize your effort and water down your fiery passion selling on eBay, it's these outrageous fees eBay charge to its sellers. It's absolutely ridiculous and if you are new on eBay, unaware of these fees before committing yourself to selling on eBay, you're sure to be discouraged and dissuaded, no question and no doubt. The first time I attempted selling on eBay, I sold an item but never make a dime out of it. In fact, I ended up loosing money on it. The item was a drop ship item, my profit on it was supposed to be $12.00. EBay charged me $13.00 for the final value fee, pay-pal charged me almost $4.00 for using their checkout services (which of course you have to use if you were to by or sell and item on eBay). These 2 outstanding fees, added to the listing fees eBay charged, put me at a huge loss. I was completely discouraged from selling on eBay, had to back out and stayed out for a while for the next 2.5 years before getting motivated again, and this time with a little more understanding about how eBay works than I initially had.

Final value fee is completely different from the **listing**

fees. It is the fee eBay charges on an item when it sales. The percentage depends on the category and the auction format but generally it's about 9% of the total sales amount, purchase and shipping.

Subtitle Fee: The title is free and you can only type in 80 characters in the field to introduce your item with pictures to potential buyers and for the search engine. However, if you think you won't be able to describe you item in 80 characters or less, additional option is available to you for a fee (20 Cent), so you can add few more info to your title description.

Additional Pictures Fee: When uploading pictures of your item that display with your title description, a maximum of 12 pictures is allowed. The first picture you upload is free, and 15 Cent for any additional uploads. However the pictures are free for certain categories like **'Collectibles',** although from their most recent newsletter, I think eBay has plan of dropping the additional picture upload fees to allow seller upload up to 12 pictures of their items for free. The secret in understanding how eBay works is paying attention, learning from your past mistakes, and most importantly reading in between lines whenever you performing any activity on eBay because everything you need to know is there in fine prints. You don't have to use any additional subtitle, the title description is enough and can do the job excellently if you know the right word to use in giving short description of your item. For instance, if you are listing men's gold watch, Seiko, brand new. This is how you should describe it in the title: **'Men's gold wrist watch Seiko brand, new!** Instead of: **'Men's dress accessory for nice elegant look'**. The last title description will yield zero result with the search engine but the first mentioned all the right words that properly describe your item to both customers and search engines.

Auction Duration Fee: EBay auction duration is somewhere between 1 to 10 days. If you choose you duration pass 7 days, you will be charged. I think seven days auction duration is long enough to get any valuable item sold with a good description. Your goal should be to eliminate as many fees as possible.

'Buy It Now' feature fee: Whenever you are doing any auction listings, you have the option of using the 'Buy It Now' feature. This means writing your starting bid price and 'buy it now' price which suppose to be at least the sum of the starting bid price and it's 10%. For example, if your starting bid price is $20, if you want to use the 'buy it now' feature, the minimum price you will put for that will be $22 (starting bid price - $20 + its 10%, that's ten percentage of $20 - $2), however, it can be more, the price you list your item is your choice. 'Buy It Now' feature provides buyers with the option of purchasing the item right away without bidding or waiting for the auction to end. So it's either you bid on the item starting with the bidding price, top the currently bidder or just buy it right away at the 'buy it now' price.

Insertion Fee: Insertion fee simply put, is, in a nutshell, the fee eBay charge you to publish your listing on eBay or rather, make it available to sellers and buyers to view. You might as well call it auction publishing fee. If your item never sold at the end of the auction duration and you wish to re-list the same item again, 'as is' without any modifications or serious changes especially in the category you originally listed, you will be waived an insertion fee. Though it might show as being charged to you but when the item sells, you will automatically get the insertion fee back. Whether the item sells or not the second time you re-list it, if you wish to re-list it again and again, you will be charged full insertion fee. Insertion fee could be less for fixed price listing. What you pay for your insertion fee is determined by the amount you're selling your item as typed in the price field. The larger the amount, the larger the insertion fee. The smaller the fixed price, the smaller the insertion fee. The best way to avoid these fees and a few others is to utilize your 50 free auction style listing which eBay gives to every seller each month and it comes with free 'buy it now' feature. This means that each month, as long as your item is not performing below eBay seller standard, you will be entitled to list 50 items, auction style free without any listing fees or 'buy it now' feature fees. However, other fees apply; like the final value fees and the rest of them. The free listings are for seven days maximum auction duration, anything more incurs you a fee. Like I said earlier, seven day auction is enough to get your item sold with a good eBay ad.

Gallery Plus Fee: This feature displays the picture of your item to potential buyers or viewers searching to buy in that category.

Extra Exposure Fee: This is the fee eBay charges you if you want your item to be seen on eBay UK or other international eBay sites.

There are many other fees eBay charges to sellers, those mentioned above are both basic pre-dominant fees and apply to every eBay seller, whether you're a pro or a novice. Understanding how eBay applies these fees and getting a handle on how to reduce or even eliminate those, makes you and effective and a better informed seller. I want to use this opportunity to assert that it's absolutely impossible to completely avoid every fee on eBay or totally eliminate them, but you can reduce or avoid some of them by following the advice already given in this book. Some of these features are unnecessary and does little or nothing in the chances of your item being sold. Use basic features but be sure to make a killer ad description to go with those.

If you follow suit on the instructions I laid out in here, you will make a lot of money on eBay by selling what's on demand, drop-shipping it without keeping any inventories, making killer ad and avoiding unnecessary fees. Take good advantage of the free auction style listings you have each month. Every now and then eBay gives some incentives by announcing upfront some upcoming free auction style listings. However, some restrictions apply, as the case with those seller accounts that performs below seller standard. This is why, like I previously said, you should always work on your feedback rating from your customers, try satisfying your customers so they may give you positive feedback which is the express lane to improving your seller performance rating. HAPPY EBAYING. DON'T FORGET TO TELL YOUR SUCCESS STORIES SO IT CAN MOTIVATE SOMEONE ELSE TO SUCCESS.

18. CONCLUSION: BONUS TIPS!

TEN MISTAKES MOST EBAY SELLER MAKE

1. Unnecessary listing fees
2. Not including pictures
3. Writing one-sentence description or nothing
4. Not accepting or using pay-pal checkout
5. Misspelling titles (wouldn't show on the search engine)
6. Desperate to sell your items, even when you loosing profit on it
7. Not answering questions from potential sellers
8. Not setting the minimum acceptable price as starting bid on your item
9. Acting as a big corporation instead of a real person, buyers like dealing with a real person when buying on eBay and not a big corp.
10 Playing low price game with other sellers. Forget the price others are selling, make good ads and write excellent descriptions to attract buyers no matter your price difference, and striving for positive feedbacks from your buyers.

GOODLUCK!!!!!!

ABOUT THE AUTHOR

Mr. M Muoghalu is 38 year-old male, an active student of RCCC, Concord NC and a full-time financially independent businessman. He was born to Mr. & Mrs. Simon Nwabugwu Muoghalu of Umuikpa Ihite Azia, Ihiala L.G.A in Anambra State of Nigeria.

He majored in 4-year undergraduate course in philosophy (B.Phil) at B.M.S Enugu and relocated to the United States of America in 2002 where he currently resides, and attended few schools; from Fordham University, Bronx, New York to Kenrick-Glennon College, St. Louis Missouri and the RCCC, Concord North Carolina where he's currently an active student.

Is it possible to be a student and a successful business person? The answer is 100%, yes. Armed with the tools of the successfully explosive world of online businesses today and knowledge of the limitless financial possibilities with the online retail giant, EBAY, the author has achieved amazingly, a financial success and independence even as a student.

He's offering similar opportunity in this book to anyone willing and ready to re-write their financial history in the easiest way possible.

'The only good is knowledge and the only evil is ignorance'   -Socrates

www.ingramcontent.com/pod-product-compliance
Lightning Source LLC
Chambersburg PA
CBHW071227170526
45165CB00003B/1016